WHIMSICAL
Times

WHIMSICAL *Times*

Memories from Hong Kong

MUKTA ARYA

PARTRIDGE

A Penguin Random House Company

To order additional copies of this book, contact
Toll Free 800 101 2657 (Singapore)
Toll Free 1 800 81 7340 (Malaysia)
orders.singapore@partridgepublishing.com

www.partridgepublishing.com/singapore

About the Author

Mukta Arya, born and raised in India, now lives in Hong Kong, where she works for a multi-national bank as human resources professional. She is the author of two collections of poetry: *Wanton Thoughts* and *3:15 pm—Musings in Hong Kong.*

Dedication

I would like to dedicate this collection of memories to the vibrant city of Hong Kong, which not only made me discover a part of myself, which was hitherto unknown to me but also gave me tremendous opportunities for introspection and reflection on life in general.

This collection would not have been possible, if my ex-manager from Ogilvy and Mather –Kalpana Rao had not told me to "jot down my first impressions of Hong Kong", during my farewell party in Mumbai. Her words remained with me when I moved to Hong Kong and motivated me to write my "first impressions" and "thoughts".

Introduction

After I moved to Hong Kong in April 2010, a variety of thoughts related to life bubbled up in my mind, and I jotted them down at that point in time. Now, when I look back, it gives me great pleasure to relive these wonderful moments. The memories have been gathered into *Whimsical Times*, which is often cheery but sometimes profound.

The memories are in the form of my "Electronic Diary" entries, written between 2010 and 2012. This was the time during which I was still "new" in Hong Kong. The places, things and events in Hong Kong during those 2 years (and even now) triggered my thought process to connect seemingly unrelated things in my life.

For those of you, who live in Hong Kong, or have lived here in the past, the memories may re-kindle the love for this magnificent place.

Monday, April 26, 2010

In a New World

I just moved to Hong Kong from Mumbai. This is my first time living on my own in a different country. I don't remember feeling any anxiety or apprehension when I arrived at the Hong Kong airport, when I entered my new office for the first time, or when I first went out in search of groceries. Strangely, it just seemed natural to stay in a serviced apartment, buy staples for my meals, and go to the office every day as if I were in Mumbai (the only difference being that my office is just a ten-minute walk from my temporary abode and I sometimes do miss driving). However, the only difference I felt was in walking (as in walking and walking) and the impracticality of my block heels and the diminished value of Indian Rupee. Otherwise, I feel as if I have been here for ages. The cosmopolitan nature of the country, the happening eating joints, the pubs, and the general buzz make it just the right place to be. With the help of my friend Reena and her husband Kshitij, it is just so easy to fit in.

I was just reflecting on this and wondering if things would have been different if I had moved when I was twenty-five, not travelled to few other countries, had not known my boss here, or if a few of my colleagues were not known to me. Perhaps it would have been a completely different experience.

For now, I look forward to aimlessly roaming around on weekends (as I have to earn my living during weekdays), soaking in the atmosphere, and settling in.

Friday, May 7, 2010

Life after Mumbai

It has been two weeks in Hong Kong, and it seems as though I have been here for ages. The transition from Mumbai to Hong Kong has been remarkably smooth, and life is running along as if nothing has changed. There are few things I do miss, such as the office boys bringing tea or coffee or even lunch to my desk. Here, I have to go to the pantry and make my own coffee. And let me tell you – it doesn't taste good at all. I especially miss calling Mr Gad (our office security guard in Mumbai) in the mornings and evenings and requesting him to order a sandwich or sev-puri. I miss my friends, colleagues, and family … and driving long distances. I miss my faithful car where I could scatter all my belongings (purse, laptop, documents, lunchbox, umbrella, and the like) and be carefree. (Since I walk to work, I have to careful about what I carry.)

Other than the above, it's quite cool, and I love the vibrant atmosphere (similar to Mumbai). I get up just in time to reach office at nine each morning (after showering, of course). I reach office and try to gather the energy to get breakfast and coffee and get down to work. My colleagues are quite warm and friendly, and my boss is a delight to work with! Lunch is usually out, and it's interesting to try different types of cuisine every day with different colleagues. So far, I have eaten Chinese (including Sichuan), Japanese (also a number of times), Malay, and Nepalese food, and I must admit that each had its own plus points. The multicultural environment is also very fascinating, and I am looking forward to working with people with different views and accents. Our HR team also has a mix of nationalities, and I was very surprised when one of them (I always thought he is Chinese) started talking in Hindi. He then revealed that he is from Nepal!

Other than that, the evenings are sometimes out in the watering holes of Hong Kong, looking at apartments to rent, or hanging out at my serviced apartment (which I am getting quite attached to). I do cook sometimes or grab some eatables from a supermarket or 7-Eleven. That's usually my dinner. Saturdays are spent roaming around (mostly window shopping, which sometimes results in real shopping), getting some grocery shopping done, or just lazing around and surfing online. My Indian friend and her husband often invite me to their house or to a movie and dinner, which I quite look forward to. Some of the Indian staff in my workplace also have started conversing with me, and one Parsi colleague told me that there are close to 200 Parsis and an agiary and a community centre for Parsis in Hong Kong.

I have also seen two movies in two weeks, which is much more than I used see in Mumbai.

In addition, I think that I will have to switch to low-heeled or flat shoes as walking in heels has gotten to be very painful.

Saturday, May 29, 2010

Apartment Hunting and Moving In

I must say that my apartment hunting and moving in experience in Hong Kong has been moved quickly. I was surprised at the speed with which everything got accomplished.

Staying for one month in the serviced apartment was very convenient and comfortable, but after a while, I longed to move into an apartment where I had enough space and the liberty to arrange and decorate it as I wished.

The whole process of getting a broker (through a friend of mine), shortlisting, and looking at apartments took just five days. The flat I liked (of the four I saw) and eventually moved into was the one I couldn't see at the designated time. I was late for the survey, and the building security did not allow visitors after six-thirty. I guess the vibe from the place was strong enough that I went back next day to see it. I entered the flat, and the first thing that caught my eye was the living and dining room with a balcony that looked onto Victoria Harbour. Seeing that and the crazy lights (like spotlights in a theatre) as well as the big cabinets, my heart made the decision, then and there. The negotiations, finalizations, and contract signing happened in the next ten days, and I was in! My house agent was quite quick and efficient. My landlady is quite gracious, and she did throw in extra things in our deal (a carpet and a massage chair). I was very delighted to meet her as she is a hair stylist and has a salon not far from my apartment. That sorted my problem of looking for a good salon, as she is quite good at her job.

I moved into my cosy little apartment (what else can I afford in the spiralling real estate market in Hong Kong?), and I quite enjoy looking at the rooms from different angles and trying to visualize what more I need. While walking in the market area, my eyes automatically go to home decor shops (they never interested me earlier). Also very strange for me is my tendency of not shopping for clothes or shoes, but rather saving money for that exotic piece of home decor. Moving into the house also made me aware of the necessity of buying certain basic things (for instance, washing powder, bath mats, toilet rolls, knives, dish cleaner, and more that I forgot in my initial shopping and never gave second thoughts to when I was living with my parents. Every day after I moved in, I would think of something I needed. Luckily, I have a supermarket five minutes away, so I don't have to worry too much.

Along with the furnishings in place when I moved it, I did buy some local furniture after plenty of visits to furniture stores and admiring local crafts. I was so excited when my furniture arrived that I waited at the entrance of the building to see it coming. I am spending my weekend arranging things. Of course, it took some time to finalize my purchases after bargaining (I do think I got a good deal), but every minute was worth it!

Now, I get up in the morning and remind myself that I have to buy a vacuum cleaner and plastic bags for my dustbin. Today being a holiday, I will have to do this necessary shopping. Off I go.

Wednesday, June 16, 2010

A Glimpse of Rural Life in Hong Kong

Sometimes, it's nice to take a break from the hustle and bustle of big cities and step back to appreciate the life in a different setting. I recently got this opportunity to go to a fishermen's village in Hong Kong as a part of the CSR activity in Societe Generale, Hong Kong. The village Tai O is near the Hong Kong airport, and we had to cross a hilly region and forest to reach it. The experience was quite interesting.

The village, though much more advanced than Indian villages in terms of amenities, exhibited the same kinds of traits in so much as the residents having a close-knit community, having a colourful environment, enjoying of small things in life, and being fit population (because of the manual interventions required in everyday life).

The journey by bus was amusing as the passengers were quite tickled to see cows grazing (coming from India, it was not an unusual sight for me). The ups and down of the roadway and sudden appearance and disappearance of sea and mountains kept us entertained.

We had gone to distribute rice dumplings (ahead of the Dragon Boat Festival on 16 June) to the elderly of Tai O Village in Hong Kong. Though the village is a tourist attraction, our foray with a local charity organization made us walk through the lanes and houses distributing the rice dumplings to the elderly. We went with red bags in hand, knocking on the doors of the elderly registered, and handing over the bag. I am sure it would have been more rewarding if most of us knew Cantonese, but all the recipients were very welcoming of the foreigners (apart from one from Hong Kong, we had volunteers from France, India, and Singapore). We saw the small prayer area outside each home and found that all of them like to put up pictures of their near and dear ones all over the walls. Some have pictures on their doors to ward off evils. We were also informed that red is considered lucky, and the bags should not be white as that colour is considered inauspicious.

We were careful not to take pictures as some of them feel that camera is an evil machine. The houses on stilts were quite interesting, with almost 100 years of being in water, and the elderly seemed quite fit as they walked around, travelled on bicycles, and jumped in and out of boats. The residents do not lock their houses.

We also went for a boat ride to see local sites – a rock resembling a frog and (luckily) a dolphin jumping out of water. The school till higher secondary looked quite good to me, and local charities had made places for wheelchairs to be parked in special enclosures in various parts of the village as the village has quite a population of quite a few elderly residents.

The seafood variety, which was displayed in the wet market, was amazing, with mind-boggling costs going up to 25,000 HKD for a delicacy.

Shirley, who was a resident of Tai O Village and the volunteer for the local charity, told me that she loves staying in the village. Even though Hong Kong is nearby, she and her friends love their place too much to leave. She even took us to her house, which was done up quite nicely in wood. The backyard of all the houses had a common passageway to pass through.

We also met an interesting lady who, while doing research on Tai O, fell in love with the place and started a free museum filled with artefacts and items depicting the history of the village. She had written a book about Tai O as well, which we bought to support her mission. Her passion for the place was very moving.

We then went to a small eating place where there were pictures of the owner's family all over the walls. It was quite a family setting, and we felt as if we had gone to someone's house for lunch. The most adorable thing was the menu that had pictures of the dishes drawn by the four-year-old grandchild of the owner. They were stuck on the wall in the eatery.

Though it was extremely hot and humid that day, and I guess my skin colour became a shade darker, the visit left me (and I am sure my colleagues) with fond memories.

Monday, June 28, 2010

Compassion and Kindness in Hong Kong via a Locked Door

Everyone writes about how heartless and cold big places are, but experiences sometimes prove otherwise. I had a similar experience that I wanted to document on my blog, as it really pulled my heartstrings.

Having spent two months with my colleagues in Hong Kong, I was actually quite moved by their concern and helpful nature when I was locked out of my office cabin with my purse and keys inside. (I know it's stupid, but my spare set of house keys was also in the same purse.)

It was eight-thirty in the evening, and many of my colleagues had gone home. The next day was a public holiday, and that's what made it all the more complicated. I was wondering what to do if we couldn't manage to get the cabin open. Luckily, I had my phone in my hand. I called my Indian friends Reena and Kshitij, who were very welcoming in inviting me to stay the night with them. However, with the help of the few colleagues remaining (Carmen and Vivien), we managed to contact our boss' assistant, Frances, who keeps duplicate keys of all cabins. She actually came at around nine-thirty that evening to give me the keys. Alas, the duplicate keys for my cabin were not in her file, as I had both the keys locked inside!

In the meanwhile, one of my other colleagues (Xavier) tried to open the lock (as he is an engineer by training). I also disturbed my boss who was concerned and told me to call a locksmith. One of my colleagues Mathieu gave me some cash in case I needed it. We contacted admin and sent an email, but since the next day was a public holiday, a lot of people had gone out of Hong Kong. I finally got a reply at eleven (the admin head kept in touch with me to see if I needed help, but by that time, Frances and Kelvin (very helpful), who was working late, had already called a locksmith to work on the lock. I must say that the locks in our office are pretty secure, and it was difficult to break the double- or triple-lock system.

The locksmith took an hour and a half to open the door. Since the locksmith spoke only Cantonese, my Chinese colleagues were of great help. Joy, who was visiting from the Singapore office, came to keep me company. Finally, the door opened at half past midnight, and we all heaved a sigh of relief.

I was so touched by the help and concern of my colleagues (whom I had known for only the past few months) that I actually had tears of gratitude in my eyes. These gestures make me feel that humanity is still alive and kicking in this seemingly selfish world.

Monday, June 28, 2010

Racing with the Dragons

The Dragon Boat Festival in June reminded me of the colourful festivals in India. It was my first time witnessing this festival, and it was quite a sight.

Dragon boat races are traditionally held as part of the annual Duanwu Festival observance in China. Nineteenth-century European observers of the racing ritual, not understanding the significance of Duanwu, referred to the spectacle as a dragon boat festival. This is the term that has become known in the west. Duanwu is observed and celebrated in many areas of east Asia with significant populations of ethnic Chinese living there (including Singapore, Malaysia, and greater China).

My colleagues and I went early morning to Stanley Beach on Hong Kong Island to see the race, which is part of the tradition. A number of companies had their teams ready for the race. Societe Generale had two teams – one had quite a few girls. Training for the race is not easy. The participants practice for months before the race, almost twice a week.

The beach was packed with the teams in their booths as well as the spectators. It was very humid and hot that day, with sudden bursts of showers, but the enthusiasm of the participants and the crowd milling about was unparalleled.

The boats shaped like dragons were used for the race with teams taking part in many rounds. One person on the boat was responsible for rhythmically beating the drums. I thought the job was easy, but it seems it was as tiring as that of rowers.

We then went to the beachfront to have breakfast and lingered in Stanley Market (and shopped a bit). The crowd from the race spilled over to the market after the race was over. Again, I felt I was in India and sometimes ended up speaking Hindi while bargaining.

The festival gave us a glimpse into the culture and tradition of Hong Kong.

Monday, June 28, 2010

A Twist Here and a Turn There

It's amazing how some shops manage to create things that are innovative and completely different from the stereotypical images of things we have. For me, home decor is my current passion, and it's a new experience. Hence, I am writing on this very fascinating topic.

While exploring Hong Kong, one comes across small and big shops hidden away. These are a delight for someone who enjoys little twists and turn in life. I saw doorstops with mice, crosses, keys, tubes, and golfer themes. Depending on your wild imagination, life in these shops is wildly imaginative and creative. I am sure the items must be coming alive at night and dancing with each other.

Discovering these places has really widened my thinking about furniture and home decor. On weekends, I love puttering around in these shops and marvelling at the creativity of the designers. Just a little twist makes a boring piece of furniture an amusing work of art. Use a different material, and it opens a whole new possibility of different designs. Inspiration by nature makes inanimate objects much more fun.

I guess that's what some people do with life. A little bit of maverick thinking and deviation from the straight and narrow path of life makes every moment becomes much more enjoyable. After all, we have only one life.

Sunday, July 4, 2010

Diving into Cultural Depths

I think the best way to understand the culture of a new place for an employee of a corporate is to participate in CSR (Corporate Social Responsibility) activities of the company. Of course, you need to really believe in the cause, but once that is settled, it's the right beginning for interesting discoveries about the place one is going to stay in for some time.

The CSR activities (at least what I have experienced) makes one meet local people from different walks of life in a friendly atmosphere. Once the connection is made, even language ceases to be a barrier. As a tourist or someone trying to discover places on his or her own, the reach cannot be as deep as the one in which a person is required to be with the local people for almost half a day.

In my experience, the beneficiaries appreciate the time devoted to their cause. For the newcomer to the country, it's an uninhibited view of how people behave, communicate, laugh, and interact with each other. It may take a little bit of effort to break the ice, but it does break and then the experience becomes very enjoyable.

From my bank, I got the opportunity today to take part in Project Thanks. We participated in an outing of children of single parents in Hong Kong to a Chinese garden where a treasure hunt was organized. Though very few of them spoke English, the children and their parents made quite a lot of effort to speak to me in English. I guess they also found it amusing to talk to someone from a different nation. Like children in any country, communicating while playing with them made things easier. The local people were very friendly and helpful. While travelling with them on the train to reach the garden – and then later during the treasure hunt, it felt as if I was among people I had known for ages.

Also, the coordinator from the NGO, Happy Teens Club, gave the background of the communities that are the beneficiaries of their efforts and also about the government support being given to certain sections of society. The area where we gathered in the morning also had its own interesting fact, which I am sure cannot be captured in any guidebook for Hong Kong.

Moral of the story: Pursue your passion for social work while working and get an interesting bonus in the form of cultural discovery of the place you live in.

Monday, August 2, 2010

Indian Dance Mania in Hong Kong

I am not a passionate dance lover, so it was very amusing for me to know that my boss, who is of Singapore Chinese descent, has been learning Bollywood dancing for quite some time in Singapore. In Hong Kong, she is learning Kuchipudi. She has graceful movements, and the steps are performed quite expertly. When she gave me the opportunity to attend an Indian dance show for charity organized by her dance master, curiosity got the better of me, and I went along on a Saturday evening to the event in Mongkok.

There was a packed house for the show, which was organized to raise funds for visually impaired children in India, and the majority of the audience was Chinese. You should have seen the frenzy when the dance masters came on stage. The dancers on stage were Chinese performing Katha (visualize dance numbers from Bollywood movies) and Kuchipudi. Imagine Kuchipudi as a sought-after dance form in Hong Kong. I was totally floored by how much these dance teachers have managed to spread Indian art and culture here. Of course, the majority of the students were females, but we did witness two Chinese guys too dancing to Bollywood numbers. The Chinese girls looked quite nice in Kathak and Kuchipudi dresses with bindis, bangles, and more.

The event managed to garner 160,000 HKD from the sale of the tickets, and for me, it was an eye-opener. I guess it takes someone from the outside to make one aware of her own rich cultural heritage.

Saturday, August 7, 2010

If There's No Option

Why do people say that something can't be done or that something is not possible? My experience shows that for a particular issue, if you have only one (and only one) option, you will end up doing it, no matter how difficult or impossible it may seem at first.

For example, I never thought I would do any of the following, and I also told everyone who would care to listen that even if this were a matter of life and death, I will never do these things.

Wear flat shoes (except for conditions such as fracture).
Use public transport or walk from work.
Cook food occasionally.
Actually forget the taste of tea with milk.
Enjoy going directly home in the evenings after work.
Take and bring back my laundry from the shop.
Carry groceries from the supermarket to my house

Three months after I moved to a new country, though, I am doing all of the above, simply because I have no option. Believe me, I tried other options, but finally, I was left with only one, and the tasks did not seem impossible at all.

I can't wear high heels all the time. In the mornings, I don't get cabs (and I am too lazy to call cabs in advance), so I have to take a bus if I want to reach office on time. Sometimes, the cabs are not available during peak hours so I have taken to walking (taking MTR means more walking). Walking is not so bad, and I don't need to spend money in a gym. As they say, after three months, any regular activity becomes a habit, so now I am used to walking. I do have to make visits to the supermarket, so if I have to survive, I pay a quick visit to these places and of course carry all the stuff myself. I also try my hand at cooking because I am sometimes too lazy to go out and eat, and I need to eat something to survive. To my surprise, I discovered that I am not too bad at cooking and am even able to eat what I cook.

My favourite example? I could not survive without at least ten cups of tea with milk in a day in Mumbai. Here, because there's no one to make it for me. I now drink green tea, Chinese tea, or coffee without milk and sugar.

So hat's off to the one who researched and discovered the insight that nothing is impossible.

A Charming Era of Celluloid

While browsing through stacks of music and movies in the music store-HMV for a DVD of songs for a friend, I stumbled across some long-forgotten but interesting movies – a whole collection of Audrey Hepburn's movies – and couldn't resist buying some. While watching her movie *Paris When it Sizzles* with Richard Holden, I was left marvelling at how such a simple plot was so dexterously converted into an engaging spectacle. After all the blood and gore and some futuristic films on HBO and the like, watching this movie from an earlier era was a delight.

The charming Audrey played the role so effortlessly and elegantly (her clothes, shoes, accessories, and hair – everything – spelled classy) that it was no surprise that Richard Holden fell for her. In some of the scenes, she tried to portray the image of a vamp, but I guess she just could not look like a bad girl. Paris looked amazing in the black-and-white shots zooming in and out and capturing its beauty. Who says technology can make or break everything? You can get the desired effect with subtle manipulation and great conversation as this film demonstrated.

The dialogue in the movie was so captivating that I was hanging on to each word. When the movie ended, I was trying to remember the last time I actually paid full attention to a movie.

It left me wondering whether I belonged to a bygone era or if the movies now are just not so charming anymore.

Sunday, September 5, 2010

Toughest Thing to Do!

I am an eternal optimist in all walks of life. Whatever the situation, I feel as though there is always a way out and that there's always a proverbial silver lining somewhere on the horizon. With this thinking, I was quite surprised to discover that for me to forgive someone (for the intentional action/s that were not exactly favourable to me) is a tough thing.

As per the books such as *Don't Sweat the Small Stuff*, we should let go of some things. It is beneficial for both us and everyone surrounding us. This looks good on paper, but it is very difficult to put into practice. Human emotions and logic wreak havoc in such situations. Even if it is tough, after some self-talk, talking with someone else, or just writing your feelings, it does become easy. After the first time, things may not be tough at all.

As Lewis B. Smedes said, "To forgive is to set a prisoner free and discover that the prisoner was you."

Sunday, September 12, 2010

The Bond of Love

The relationship between parents and their children is so precious. I got a chance to witness the bond for a few precious hours, when along with other volunteers, I attended Societe Generale-supported CSR activity in Hong Kong. It was the closing ceremony of Project Thanks, where the children from underprivileged (low-income/single-parent) families had earned some money over a period of few months. On the last Saturday, they gave gifts bought with the earned money to their parents/grandparents.

In a ceremony that was attended by almost 200 children and parents and guardians (in spite of heavy rains), we witnessed children proudly presenting gifts. The gifts were well-thought-out by the kids and bought with the help of Happy Teens Club and Societe Generale. The parents and grandparents were so proud and happy of their children. It was an emotional moment for them and us, seeing so much affection in that room.

It's also poignant in an age where we have so many stories floating around about children neglecting their parents and sending them to old-age homes. These young children bring home a message for all of us to value those who have given us birth and shaped our lives.

Thursday, September 23, 2010

Coincidence

It was the day of mid-autumn festival eve in Hong Kong and coincidentally the final day of Ganapati Visarjan in Mumbai. The offices in Mumbai let employees leave early on that day, and in Hong Kong, the employees were allowed to leave at four the same day. I just couldn't help marvelling at the parallel.

Hong Kong buildings and houses were decorated with lamps that reminded me of the kandeels in India during Diwali. The festival of light was very much the same except that the lights were electric here and firecrackers were not allowed to be burnt by everyone. I also bought a goldfish lantern to hang in my apartment.

Business partners and friends were presenting fruits, dry fruits, and moon cakes to corporate partners. Like in India, fruits, dry fruits, and sweets are distributed during Diwali.

The initial part of the fire-dragon dance also reminded me of the Pooja, which is done during some of the festivals in India. The noise, the crowds, and the police teams containing the crowds give me a feeling of *deja vu*.

It made me realize (with more emphasis) that we may belong to different parts of the world, differentiated by borders, language, and skin colour, but deep down, the cultures of all the countries are probably based on the same foundation.

Thursday, September 23, 2010

So Little Time

Time flies. This is accentuated by the fact that there are so many things to do and so little time for it (especially when it is travelling at a break-neck speed). Still, most of us waste these precious moments thinking about irrelevant things, petty things which bring no joy to our lives.

For me, part of the list is:

Visit exotic places (at least once a year).
Bungee jumping (at least once).
Write a crazy and mad novel (before I turn thirty-seven).
Read the latest and the old novels, books, and stories.
Finally start the morning jog.
Manage to have fruit cocktails three days in a week.
Manage to keep my cupboard well-organized three days in a row.
Find an occasion to wear to the new dress, which I am sure will look good.
Go on a spa holiday, and do nothing but pamper myself,
Sing in tune when we go for karaoke.
Develop a taste for fish.
Drink black coffee without sugar.
Walk faster than Hong Kong office goers in the mornings and not slow down as the end of travellator zooms in the horizon.

Not scatter my DVDs around, and keep them in their proper place.

Read the books I have bought but abandoned after few pages.

Stop wasting time on inconsequential things, and make sure you get at least fifty percent of little things done. The pleasure derived from accomplishing your list of little things, I assure you, will be priceless.

Sunday, September 26, 2010

Stand-Up Comedy

Have you ever seen a stand-up comedy act? For me, Friday night act was the first in my life. I had read about it in novels and was not exactly excited about stand-up comedy. Most of the parts I read told of flat jokes and no laughter. Also, the fact that comedy is the hardest thing for a person to carry out made me wonder how the comedians would connect with a walk-in audience.

I stumbled upon it in Hong Kong while organizing a public speaking course with First Finance using stand-up comedy as a base. Since the trainers, Anthony Solimini and Jameson (Jamie) Gong, and the owner of the comedy club (Take-Out Comedy on Elgin Street) were performing that night (and they invited all the participants), curiosity got the better of me and I landed at the show (a bit apprehensive). The stage was set with orange curtains (a small stage for the comedian), and the audience surrounded the stage from three sides.

Jamie came on stage with a natural ease and started chatting with the audience, involving some of them and making fun. Surprisingly, the jokes and humour didn't sound offensive at all. There were five other comedians (diversity was even there, one Italian, one American, one Chinese, and two Indians), and all of them were amazing. The jokes elicited lots of laughter, and even though they were picking on some of the audience (including me), it was just hilarious. I don't think I have ever laughed so much. The comedians were at ease with the audience, and their deliveries were awesome. The jokes were contemporary, and some of us could feel the connection with what they were saying. There were two female comedians, one Chinese and one Indian, and their delivery was quite powerful. The topics were interesting without being derogatory.

Having gone there once, I am sure I would love to go there again and again. Thanks, Anthony and Jamie, for showing me the lighter side of life.

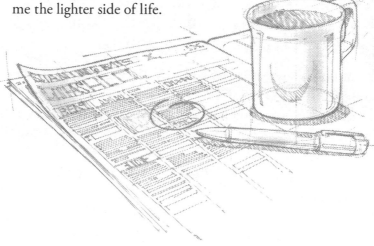

Saturday, October 9, 2010

Unstructured

I am great fan of unstructured clothes, furniture, stationery, and haircuts, but the lack of structure in all the aforementioned things in Hong Kong is mind-boggling.

Let me first describe the clothing, which is my favourite subject. The layers over layers and the unsymmetrical cuts are really very interesting. Sometimes, you even get lost wearing the various layers. The cuts and the layers are juxtaposed in such a way that the same set can be worn two or three different ways. I actually saw a set which you can wear five different ways. All very nice, you may say, as they are actually designed for the thin Hong Kong girls on whom all these strange cuts look amazingly stylish. So the girl in the shop who was exhibiting the style looked good in each of the five styles. In these shops of small designers, you can actually find excellent design at throwaway prices. As with everything, you will have to search for them in some unsuspecting areas.

Some of the really strange cuts I saw in clothes shops were tops with a funny tail coming out of one side, one sleeve missing with other sleeve adorned with chains and stones, and a sheath giving one a look of a strange gladiator.

However, with careful selection (and avoiding the extremes), you can put together a look that is unconventional and trendy. One can actually spend a whole day doing nothing but looking at the enormous creativity of assorted minds. Try it – it might turn out to be fun.

Saturday, October 9, 2010

What's in a Name?

Every country has its share of traditional and cute names. In Hong Kong, some of the names are so cute that they just get imprinted in the long-term memory.

Crystal, Cindy, Vicky, Frances, Grace, Keith, Raymond, Grace, and Helen are quite widespread. However, I was struck by some uncommon names (maybe not uncommon in Hong Kong and China) that I found to be cute. Here are the names that I still remember.

Fruity names: Apple and Orange
Drink and food names: Milk, Coffee, and Bread
Country/city names: German and Sydney
Colour names: Blue and Red
Season/weather/time-of-day names: Dawn, Snow, Sunny, and Icy
Character names: Pinocchio, Tweety, and Twiggy
Other names: Prudence, Bell, Substance, Fishee, Fan, Dream, Rainbow, Kinki, Kitty, and Kit

I am sure I will come across more names that will remain with me forever and remind me that life can spring surprises in something as basic as names.

Sunday, October 24, 2010

Shining Pates

If you let your eyes wander idly over a crowded area in Hong Kong, you will definitely be accosted by the sight of a sprinkling of bald heads in the sea of people. The shaved, gleaming heads proclaim to the world that baldness can be quite attractive.

I am not suggesting that all the guys with a shining pate are follically challenged – a few of them may be. For them, being completely bald and looking like the icon of a fashionable male is much better than to trying to grow hair via endless treatments or wearing a wig. Although it may mean shaving the head regularly, that's a small price to pay.

I must admit that most of the guys do look much better bald (though some of them do resemble villains in old movies). However, sometimes, I find it difficult to distinguish between guys sporting the look. They start to all look the same.

Since the look is easy on the eyes, let the tribe grow!

Monday, November 1, 2010

Life is like Water

It's amazing how human beings adapt to changing situations with ease (after an initial two- or three-hour struggle). I came back to Mumbai after six months, and after an hour, it felt as if I never left it in the first place. The house, my room, the familiar roads, the car, the pubs, the drinks, the food, tea with milk, friends, and family – everything was like before.

It was the same when I moved to Hong Kong six months ago. After the feeling of newness had subsided, it was as if I was staying there forever. I stopped drinking milk tea (as it is too much effort) and didn't miss it at all. Now, after being in Mumbai for a week, I drink six or seven cups of milk tea per day and want more and more. I didn't miss driving in Hong Kong at all, but back here in magical Mumbai, I can't sit in the passenger seat and can drive with complete ease all day long.

I guess life, like water, takes shape of whatever vessel it is poured into.

Sunday, November 28, 2010

Unpredictability

If we all knew what's going to happen in the future, there would be no excitement left. In my opinion, the thrill of discovering the undiscovered, uncovering the covered, unveiling the veiled, and coming face-to-face with a completely unpredictable situation is what makes the world go around.

Imagine a world where what the astrologers write about comes true (to the last word) and we just follow it, knowing full well the outcome of our efforts. It would be so boring. When we don't know something, we are optimistic or pessimistic (depending on a person's orientation) and try our best to make it work. It leads to innovation in ideas and the way we do things. It keeps us on the edge, gives us purpose, makes our lives interesting and gives wings to our imagination.

Unpredictability is equally interesting in all walks of life – in movies (especially murder mysteries); dramas; presentations for new products, processes, and ideas; brainstorming sessions that provide new solutions; romantic situations where spontaneous and unpredictable reactions are much more favoured; planning holidays (when you are planning for Russia and end up in South Africa), shopping (ending up buying four dresses instead of a single shirt); salons (when you want to keep your hair long and just want a trim but try a short haircut on a whim) – the list is endless.

Life is much more interesting when it's unplanned and unpredictable, so enjoy the thrilling sensation by embracing the spontaneity of life.

Sunday, November 28, 2010

Differences

All of us are different. It's a well-known and proven fact that humans have different personalities and that their way of working and approach to life is dependent on that – some are organized, some are spontaneous, and some fall in between. As earthlings, we survive because of the complementarity of our skills, mind sets, and ways of working.

Why do we always try to change the way people work? We may have someone who is an extrovert, has no fear of speaking in public, and can come up with new ideas and also implement them, but we still may say that he is not enough process- or detail-oriented. It's very rare to find someone who can come up with unthought-of ideas and also be happy with routine tasks. These two different things require completely different mind sets and personalities. When it's proven that one person can't be all these things, we still try to find a jack of all trades.

I would think that the best strategy is to identify the positives of everyone and leverage on that in order to have satisfaction on both sides. Trying to focus too much on the deficiencies and converting them into positives is sometimes achievable, but it is much less so and takes much longer as well as additional efforts. In an organization, the best way is to find employees with complementary skills and mind sets instead of having doppelgangers.

Saturday, December 4, 2010

There's a Whole New World Out There

In moments of laziness, I sometimes want to order take-away food, shop for groceries online or by phone, and even want to shop for clothes online. However tempting that may be, I sometimes drag myself out of lethargy and go to real brick-and-mortar shops to shop for essential items (which, unfortunately or fortunately, is every week). Once I enter these shops in flesh and blood, I feel like Alice in Wonderland.

Every week, there's something new and enchanting. The variety is amazing, and I never tire of looking at differences and marvelling at the innovations. Humankind has really progressed. I spend more time in a supermarket trying to decide between two similar products. I didn't even know that there are five varieties of honey and tissue paper can also be different. The number of frozen food items amazes me, and I just wonder why people take the trouble of cooking fresh food (I'm not very fond of cooking). I must admit that I end up buying some stuff that I don't ever use, but that's the pull of in-store marketing.

I cannot tell you how satisfied I feel after my weekly trips to the supermarkets. The fact also impresses upon me that if I had fixed ideas about what I want to eat and use, I will never (and emphatically never) discover the wonderful things that FMCG companies are doling out every week. Keep an open mind, and don't be so fixed on what you like or don't like. There's a whole new world out there.

December 18, 2010

What's Your Poison?

Mine is a glass of Bellini.

I always liked fruit cocktails. Normally, I would love to have different kinds of fruitinis or vodka with orange. A visit to Venice a few years ago changed all that. When Zehera and I were on our amazing tour of Italy few years ago, the walking expedition in Venice led us to the amazing place where I had a glass of champagne with peach syrup. Zehera has champagne with strawberry syrup. With the first sip of our respective drinks, we were in heaven. These became our favourite drinks.

We came back, but our hearts were stuck on the drinks of Venice. For me, it's Bellini all the time, and I never tire of it. I have had it numerous times and in a number of places, but the Bellini from Venice (where it was invented in the Harry's Bar) remains unmatched.

Imagine my delight when I found a readymade Bellini drink in an Italian food joint in Hong Kong! It's quite good. I wonder if I will ever get tired of my poison.

Thursday, January 13, 2011

Masala Chai

Boil a cup of water. Pour it over a sachet filled with magic powder. Stir it thoroughly and voila! You have a cup of masala chai, without bothering about milk and sugar and tea. Isn't it amazing? It's nothing short of a miracle to me.

I was addicted to masala chai in Mumbai and drank at least ten cups of the sweet, milky boiled concoction every day. After I relocated to HK, I did not have access to masala chai in the office, and even at home, it didn't taste the same. So imagine my delight when my friend from Mumbai (who else but the all-knowing Zehera Mecklai) brought a big packet of sachets of masala chai powder with her. I was a bit sceptical, wondering how something as delicious as masala chai could be commercialized and powdered and sealed in small sachets. But there they were in all their glory, ready to be enjoyed.

And so I am back to my normal "milk tea sipping" mode in the cold January in HK. These small practical innovations which bring a smile to the face of mere mortals like me are really worth celebrating.

Sunday, January 16, 2011

Love Affair with Nature

Human being's love affair with nature never dies. It may fade away for a while, but it always comes back. I tend to believe that however great the progress mankind makes in creating artificial scenery, buildings, amusement parks, and shopping malls, the charm and the attraction of natural surroundings will always have the greatest pull on us.

This realization struck me quite strongly, when I went on a hiking trip to the Hong Kong Geopark in Sai Kung. The trip was full of surprises. It showcased the scenic beauty of the HK countryside, which I had not even visualized in my dreams. The mountains, the various water bodies, the vast spread of uninhibited natural beauty, the fresh air (though a bit cold), the clear skies, the winding pathway, the appearance and disappearance of exotic flora, the steep climb, the welcome downhill amidst the jungle, and the smiles on the faces of fellow hikers – all left me spell-bound.

I guess life throws us pleasant surprises when we least expect them. When we began the hike, we didn't know where we would end up. Spying a far-off dam, we thought we would never be able to make it. Imagine our surprise when we did reach the dam (East Dam) and were rewarded with the sight of waves lashing onto a cofferdam made of dolosses and rocks called "petrified waterfalls", along with some islands jutting out of the sea at interesting angles formed by erosion.

The scenic beauty of this easy hiking trail – called the MacLehose Trail – frankly cannot be described in words or captured in photographs. It must be experienced.

There are plenty of nature trails which present a really beautiful picture of Hong Kong. They also present a pleasant opportunity to start or rekindle one's love affair with nature.

Friday, January 21, 2011

Hot and Spicy

It numbs your mouth and then sets it on fire. It makes your tongue tingle – and surely not with delight. So why do so many people seek out really – and I mean *really* – hot food and flock to restaurants that specialize in it?

The Sichuan restaurant Chilli Fagara in the SoHo district of Hong Kong is one such hot spot. It was introduced to me by Reena and Kshitij on my second day in Hong Kong. With red chillies hanging overhead and a very red face with a long beard staring down at you, the restaurant has a really exotic atmosphere. The tables are closely placed, and the food is the fieriest I have ever eaten. Take one spoonful of most of the dishes, and your mouth will never forget the rendezvous with the chillies of Sichuan. The drinks include special Chilli Fagara cocktails that contain what else but chillies, combined with whichever drink you prefer.

The place is never empty, except when it's closed. Getting a table there is really difficult. What I can't understand is why, even when your nose runs continuously and eyes water unabated, people still want to go again and again. That includes me! I am unable to eat properly because of the spice in the food – in spite of being an Indian – and have to leave half of my chilli cocktail for the same reasons, yet every fifteen days, I end up eating there.

Is it the thrill of eating something challenging to the taste buds which attracts people like me to torture themselves, or something else? I am still trying to unravel it.

Amused

I am still not over my fascination with mid-air shopping options. Travelling by air from Hong Kong to various short-haul Asian locations, I occupy myself with the shopping guide, and it has never failed to entertain me, even after I've seen the same issue two or three times.

Apart from the normal collection of perfumes, watches, pens, scarves, and jewellery, some items selected for sale in-flight are amusing and even bizarre. The inventors are really worth applauding, as some of these items are practical and frankly useful.

A case in point is an advanced version of tweezers (for shaping eyebrows) called La-Tweez Pro Illuminating Tweezers. After looking at this product in the shopping guide of Cathay Pacific four or five times while travelling, I finally gave in and bought these "revolutionary" tweezers, along with their chic compact case. They have a push-button for illumination and they really work well.

I also found some really cool items that captured my imagination and brought a smile to my face. I found a tower fan which looked kind of cute, a decanter called "escargot decanter", a travel press, and a latte milk frother. There was an electric table grill on offer with a free knife and fork set, and there was an oil and vinegar set as well.

The other items which caught my attention were VIP (Very Intelligent Pocket – they seem to be things of the past), folding bicycle (I am still wondering why they will sell a bicycle mid-air), and Digital Note Taker. I guess these mid-air shops aim to gather the best of innovative things, and of course provide entertainment to travellers like me.

Finally, I was knocked out by an item which I thought was an unlikely seller: Paris Hilton ladies watch.

Life is full of surprises.

Saturday, February 12, 2011

Amazed by Everything

I read somewhere that a wise man (or woman) is amazed by everything. When you dig deeper, it probably is true for all of us. How else would we stay interested in our jobs, our day-to-day chores, the same things we all have to repeat again and again? I guess it's this ability to be amazed by everything every day that helps us in reinventing life and looking at it from a different angle.

Notice the way children climb up and down stairs. They may do it every day on the same stairs, but they still find some way of counting the steps differently, hopping with a difference in the length of stride, criss-crossing ... just coming up with different ways to go up and down. Their happiness when doing this daily task is priceless.

It's the same with some people at work. They may have done the same things for years, but with a new way of looking at their routine, they make their work life (and the work life of those who come in contact with them) pleasurable and meaningful. Otherwise, it would be easy to get bored with your job. I guess the ability to be amazed is nature's way of keeping balance.

Try to be amazed by everything around you. You will not regret it.

Saturday, February 26, 2011

Being a Dragon Boater

In June 2010, when I was a spectator at the dragon boat races at Stanley beachfront and watched teams of companies guiding their boats to their destination, I never thought that only a year later I would enter the waters of Hong Kong to paddle a dragon boat.

When Societe Generale started a third team for women (it already had two boats) for the dragon boat competition in June 2011, I enrolled, not knowing what lay in store for me. In fact, what lay in store was beyond my imagination.

We had training sessions every Saturday. I bunked the first one because of cold weather, but when I went for the second one, the excitement of paddling the boat overtook any apprehension I may have had of venturing into the rough waters of the HK sea (with a life jacket, of course). Surprisingly, I found that the rowdy wind, not-too-disciplined waves, and cold weather actually added to the excitement. For me, since it was the first time, even the paddles – which we were holding as if we were ancient Chinese warriors – were quite interesting.

The one-hour session with an instructor and the ten of us was rigorous, with plenty of strokes, a lot of water splashing, and an amazing view of the area surrounding the body of water. We also saw kites enjoying water sports to the fullest with sailing, paragliding, etc. (a few more things to add to my bucket list).

The adrenalin-pumping dragon boat race training left me feeling really great. I look forward to every Saturday when we do the same for an hour.

Saturday, February 26, 2011

An Ode to Enthusiastic Youngsters

There's so much to learn from the younger generation. Whenever I interact with youngsters (that is, people younger than me), I am always amazed by their ability to try out new things and look at the world with fresh eyes. I guess I draw my inspiration to do new things from these bundles of energy and enthusiasm.

From backpacking alone for almost four months in unknown territories to actively participating in CSR activities, to leading a dragon boat team, to hiking and walking for 100 kilometres, to skydiving almost every month, these young people I know as colleagues in Societe Generale - including Joy Lim, who backpacked alone in Europe, the United States, and Canada, and Lorene Latour, who does all the above mentioned activities regularly – have left me wondering if there's anything in this world which cannot be done. The courage, the determination, and the stretch of imagination required to make these thoughts a reality make me admire these enterprising young people.

Talking to them makes my bucket list that much longer.

Thursday, March 17, 2011

Face to Face

When you come face to face with something about which you have read since childhood, how do you feel? I am not able to define this feeling, but my heart certainly skips a beat.

I remember when I first saw the Taj Mahal almost twenty years ago, or the pyramids in Egypt two years ago – the first sight of them, hidden beneath fog on a cold morning, literally took my breath away. Standing on the Aswan Dam on the River Nile brought back memories of geography lessons in school. The Coliseum in Rome, the Leaning Tower of Pisa, and the Eiffel Tower – all brought back memories of history classes in which we would cut and paste pictures of these wonders in our notebooks and charts.

When I first stepped on the Great Wall of China last year, it was as if I had stepped into another world – one which, for me, had existed only in books and movies. It was a very unreal feeling, one that occurs not only with the monuments and structures but also with places like islands which I saw in many Hercule Poirot movies. When I found myself on one of these, the feeling was one of déjà vu.

More recently, at a flower show, I found some pitcher plants on sale. I was pleasantly surprised and also very excited, for I had read a long time ago that pitcher plants actually lure insects and kill them with their digestive juices. I thought they only grew in the wild. Seeing them just 40 HKD away was quite tempting, and I gave in to temptation. The same was the case when I saw a touch-me-not plant for the first time. It was amazing to touch it and see it droop and come back to normal.

I guess it's like realizing one of your pleasant dreams, with a light heart and a twinkle in your eye.

Friday, March 18, 2011

Bond for Life

A recent hoarding in HK displayed a message about how pets are for life and people should not have them if they have no time to care for them. This struck a chord with me, as I had seen the reality of this problem in my own house.

My sister is very fond of pets, and she has a number of them. I saw her and my nephew get attached to the pet they had at the time they moved to Mumbai. The pet dog, named Zora, grew up in their house. My nephew would get up early to take Zora out to the park, feed her, and take care of her. I was amazed at his dedication and commitment to Zora. The dog would sleep on the bed; whenever they visited us with Zora, she would not sit on the floor but would come up on the bed and lie down to relax. My room and all my black clothes would be full of white hair the next day.

I remember very clearly the day when, because of the hectic lifestyle in Mumbai and her inability to look after Zora, my sister had to finally – after delaying it for a year and trying to find an alternative – make the decision to leave Zora at our cousin's house near Delhi. I have never seen my sister and my nephew cry so much, and I did see tears in Zora's eyes too. The bond they had built with Zora over those three years was so strong that Zora was an integral part of my sister's family. They dropped Zora off at my cousin's house, in which there were many pets, and only when they saw her well settled did they return to Mumbai. I remember hearing telephone conversations between my sister, nephew, and Zora from time to time.

When human beings develop feelings for pets and are pained at the thought of parting with them, it's really very hard to withstand the separation. Be careful about who or what you allow into your world, for the relationship is for the long term.

Sunday, March 20, 2011

The Festive Spirit

I suspect festivals were invented to bring some enjoyment to people's day-to-day life. Sitting here far from India, where the festival of colours (Holi) is being played today, I actually realize the importance of some of these festivals, which I took for granted when I was there. Sometimes I would sneer at the people who were so enthusiastic about decoration, meeting relatives and neighbours, distributing presents and sweets, and dressing up on these occasions. I was so wrong to do that. These few days a year do bring all of us – who may not meet regularly because of work or distance – together to enjoy ourselves.

In HK, we have our own set of festivals, and the noise, crowds, and colourful decorations remind me that human beings – wherever they are on this planet – are basically social animals. If these diversions were not available, life would be extremely boring for all of us.

So I guess we should just let our hair down and enjoy the festivities while we can, and spread the happiness around.

Sunday, March 20, 2011

Just Do It

How do we know we can't do something if we have not tried it at all?

Not only history but everyday news and stories from television, magazines, and newspapers show us that it is completely absurd to assume that because someone has not done something in the past, he or she cannot do it in future. All inventors, scientists, athletes, chefs, other professionals, and even children believe that even if someone else failed at an attempt to do something new and different, there's no guarantee that they will fail at it too. So they just go ahead and do it – and then are feted by the same people who earlier were cautious or cynical about their achievement.

It could be as simple a thing as taking up a new sport and excelling at it, or taking up a totally unrelated job and making a success of it, or finding a new way of organizing all your clothes in an overflowing wardrobe, or even finally managing to make sure your handbag is well-organized and you are able to find things at the right moment. All of us have unused potential; in reality, we use only 20 to 30 per cent of it. Keep an open mind and just go ahead and do it. You and everyone else may be pleasantly surprised.

Sunday, March 20, 2011

Bits and Pieces

It's strange how bits and pieces of incidents stick in our memory and remain with us our whole life long. I guess whatever we find peculiar or affects us most at that time always remains. For instance, I still remember the following moments:

- following my sister Prerna on sweltering afternoons to raid fruit-laden trees and eat our "prized catch of the day" on the terrace
- learning how to cycle at the age of 8, falling down almost every day for a week, crying for almost an hour, but later on being thankful for the experience
- the amazement when I first saw the bud on a wild cactus plant at the age of almost 6, and after opening found a very attractive-looking appendage
- the first time I went with my cousins to the bank of the Yamuna River in Delhi and tried to steal a watermelon from the field on the bank, leaving my slipper behind in the process
- the first time in Haridwar, when I took my first holy dip in the cold water of the river Ganges and also placed the lit diya on a leaf and left it in water
- eating aloo-chat and other snacks with my sister while walking back from school in Kolkata
- seeing a cow gave birth to a calf right behind our school in Delhi

- the time in college in Mumbai when a roadside astrologer told me my future, and most of the things did come true
- dissecting frogs, chameleons, and cockroaches in biology practical classes and managing to locate their nervous systems
- sleeping on the cool terrace in hot weather, under the clear skies in Delhi
- going to the vegetable market with our mother so we could eat the tasty "chat" near the vegetable market
- dropping and receiving guests at the railway station so I could buy Hindi novels, which are available only at the railway-station bookstores
- going to see Aamir Khan's first movie, *Quamat se Quamat Tak*, with my entire tenth standard class and speaking about it for months afterwards
- reading my mother's women's magazines and novels at the age of 12, without her knowledge
- mountain biking in Simla and narrowly escaping being flung in the valley

The list is endless, but the memories are still there and refuse to go away.

Sunday, April 10, 2011

Sunday Afternoon Adventure

When my colleague Karen Khaw suggested a midday visit to the suburb of Hong Kong called Sham Shui Po to see the wholesale market dealing with earring and necklace components, I agreed readily, as I do love danglers. I had seen some of Karen's handiwork in the form of a nice-looking pair of danglers, but nothing could prepare me for the variety that the market had to offer. I felt like Alice in Wonderland, with each and every item in the endless line of shops casting a spell on me and my friends.

The area itself is such a contrast to Central in HK, and it showcases the vibrant life of HK people. Crowds, busy streets, old buildings, and local food everywhere – all gave a genuine feel to the place. But of course, the exciting part was the shops featuring beads of all possible sizes and colours, earring pieces (including wooden, synthetic, and stone), Swarovski crystals, chains of different designs, and anything else you can imagine to make jewellery. While selecting the ones to finally convert into actual earrings and necklaces, my brain was brimming with endless possibilities. I had been in HK for over a year and never thought I could actually be making something like danglers out of isolated pieces.

Like a first-timer, I bought a lot of pieces, and I couldn't wait to try my hand with them. I reached home and got down to business, and it was an amazing feeling to convert bits and beautiful pieces into danglers the way I liked them. When I put them on, it was like being transported to a new world of colour and design. I ended up making nine danglers of different designs and one necklace in my first attempt.

There are so many interesting things out there – we just need an introduction, and an entire new world opens up.

Sunday, May 1, 2011

Hot Pot

A simmering pot of broth sits in front of you, right in the middle of a bustling restaurant, along with a selection of raw vegetables, dumplings, and meat. You slowly slide a vegetable or meatball into the pot, watch it cook right before your eyes, and then scoop the cooked morsel into your plate or bowl. I must admit that I am not a big fan of cooking, but this scenario – from one of the "hot pot" restaurants in Wan Chai in Hong Kong – did make me feel exhilarated. It feels great to eat food you have just cooked with your own hands, as your eyes followed every moment of the cooking process.

Since I was first introduced to this amazing phenomenon by my colleague Joy Lim, I have tried to get more information about the hot pot. A traditional way of cooking, the Chinese hot pot boasts a history of more than a thousand years. The term "Mongolian hot pot" is often used, but it is unclear whether the dish actually originated in Mongolia. Hot-pot cooking seems to have spread to northern China during the Tang Dynasty (AD 618–906). In time, regional variations developed with different ingredients, such as seafood.

By the time of the Qing Dynasty, the hot pot had become popular throughout most of China. Today in many modern homes, particularly in the big cities, the traditional coal-heated steamboat or hot pot has been replaced by electric, gas, or induction versions. An amazing way of tasting local food, hot pot is a must-do for anyone exploring China.

Monday, May 2, 2011

Drawing the Parallels

Human beings are basically the same all over the world. This was made evident to me after I visited some parts of China. While exploring the historical sites and absorbing the atmosphere with the help of a tour guide, I learned a few facts about the Chinese culture and way of life that reminded me of Indian culture, including the following:

- Kings had a large number of mistresses. All lived in the harem together – and maybe fought for attention.
- The walled cities were huge and had moats around them filled with water (and crocodiles).
- For joyous occasions and celebrations, the colour red is considered an auspicious colour and black an unsuitable colour, both in China and India. White in both cultures is associated with death.
- Chinese temples are similar to those in India – in terms of the way of worshipping with incense sticks, for example.
- The flower and nature motifs on clothes and embroidery in the museum reminded me of the Indian way of life in the past.
- The utensils and jewellery again seemed to be in the same format as in India (or vice versa).

The list is endless, but history does show that the similarities cannot be ignored. The languages may seem like they're from two unrelated planets, and weather conditions may differ (and lead to different food habits and clothes), but basically, human beings are the same everywhere.

Sunday, May 8, 2011

Down Memory Lane

Narrow lanes in Wan Chai in Hong Kong in May …
weekend crowds thronging the streets for shopping …
hot humid weather with air full of different kinds of
sound … knick-knacks of all kinds imaginable (and some
you'd never think of) …

I was walking with one of my friends, just looking around, and in the middle of all the chaos, we saw an old man with a very small stall selling crochet pins of different sizes and threads of different colours and width. The unexpected sight of these pins and thread threw me back to my schooldays when, in one of the classes called SUPW (social useful productive work), we were taught interesting things like making greeting cards with oil paints, crocheting, cross-stitching, knitting, and making bags out of jute.

I enjoyed these classes very much in my schooldays. I never had a chance to do any of those things again – or I chose not to. Still, the memory of old days made me buy a crochet pin and some threads at the old man's stall.

I was not sure whether I would do anything with them, but once I sat down with them – while watching TV – my fingers started working on their own. I was delighted to find myself creating the same patterns I had known in school. I used to think that women who knitted or did similar things really had nothing else to do, but the rediscovery of crocheting made me realize that these are actually very engaging and interesting activities which allow one to create beautiful designs out of nothing.

This incident made me think that maybe my beliefs over the years need rethinking and a new way of seeing.

Sunday, May 15, 2011

Getting Used to Things

Is it possible to get used to things which one, as a person, does not believe in or finds completely disgusting? Yes, it is. I can say it with absolute certainty.

I became aware of this amazing phenomenon via TV programs. When I moved to Hong Kong a year ago, I subscribed to few Hindi channels to be in touch with India. Since I had one Hindi channel with all the daily soaps (apart from a news and music channel), I used to play it in the background after I came back from work – just to hear Hindi after working and interacting with others all day in English. In India, I remember, I would prefer not to see the Hindi daily soaps, as I found them completely disconnected from my life in Mumbai and really thought they represented drama at its worst. Now, in HK, since the Hindi channels with the soap operas play in the background every night, without meaning to I started remembering the storylines, characters, and voices of these various serials – so much so that I really waited for the next episode. It was strange, but I did find myself entangled in the complex stories of the characters.

What this tells me is that if one has no (or few) options and is subjected to it on a consistent basis, one can get used to anything – good, bad, or disgusting.

Sunday, May 15, 2011

Hello Kitty

You hear this term, and I am sure an image of a character loved by preadolescent girls comes to mind. It did to mine; that's how this brand was positioned when it launched. The reality is that (at least in Hong Kong) Hello Kitty does not only seem to have preteens in its clutches — it has women of all ages enthralled by it.

Hello Kitty seems to be everywhere — mobile phone holders, pouches, purses, travel bags, jewellery, stationery, mugs, clothes, or things like toasters, dishes, home appliances, cameras, and even cars. There's a Hello Kitty credit card cobranded with VISA, a Hello Kitty theme restaurant in Taipei, and a maternity home in Taiwan where Hello Kitty is featured on the receiving blankets, room decor, bed linens, birth-certificate covers, and nurses' uniforms. The hospital's owner explained that he hoped the theme would help ease the stress of childbirth.

I read somewhere that at one point in the 1990s; Mariah Carey adopted Hello Kitty as a fashion statement. I have nothing against the brand, but I am unable to understand how and why it snuggled into the thoughts of adults and managed to stay there. Must be something related to the child in all of us.

Sunday, June 12, 2011

Laughing Away

Yesterday night, I could not stop laughing – for almost two and a half hours nonstop. I was watching a Bollywood hit called *Ready* with Salman Khan, and I saw it on the big screen in HK (sometimes Bollywood hits are organized in cinema halls in HK).

The mindless story, the witty dialogue (really witty, although sometimes maybe a little cheesy), the catchy songs and dances, and the crazy acting left the audience in stitches. Frankly, it had been a very long time since I'd laughed so much.

It was so refreshing that even after a long day and evening, I was feeling fresh at midnight. It reminded me of the importance of humour in our lives and moments when we just need to relax and not think of anything else. Mindless entertainment is one of the best ways to remain rejuvenated. Go ahead and watch some of the Bollywood films. I guarantee you will come out happier and more relaxed.

Sunday, June 12, 2011

The Wonder Years

I met one of my classmates from my grad days recently when she was in transit from the United States to India via Hong Kong. It was a great feeling to meet someone from my distant past. We had reconnected thanks to Facebook.

Shilpa and I were batch mates while doing our B.Sc. in life science at Ruia College in Mumbai. She had gotten married and moved to the United States, and my life had taken a different direction, with an MBA. We lost touch for many years.

To catch up on those magical college days — remembering the hang-out places (the restaurant where we ate Chinese-Indian food, the tea shop with Misal Pav and Samosas), the professors (Ganesh Iyer, Rattan Kumar, Arun Kothari — the handsome one), the other batch mates and where they are now, romances between batch mates and the final result — it was like being transported back to the wonder years.

Shilpa mentioned the coincidence of having four of our batch mates from Ruia College living in the same area in California now and how they are still in touch. While chatting, we realized that each and every moment of life is so precious and important. Even so many years down the line, we understood the importance of seemingly unimportant events and activities in college.

Really, our college days were the best days – carefree and really enjoyable. I don't think they will ever come back.

Sunday, July 17, 2011

Reliving the Past

This past month has been one of reunion with old friends. I met Shilpa Palekar after thirteen years and then I met Karthika Grover after nineteen years. She was in HK with her naughty and adorable daughter Muskan for the holidays, and we met up. We studied together during our years in primary school in Delhi and kept in touch through greeting cards and letters. Later, after my parents moved to Kolkata (at that time Calcutta) and then Mumbai (at that time Bombay), we did meet a few times whenever I visited Delhi, but that was a long twenty years ago.

It was through Facebook that we reconnected after so many years. Really, it was an amazing feeling to see her and her daughter. Catching up on the various events in life – the good, the bad, and the ugly times, the present, the hope for future – was quite wonderful. In hindsight, everything looks much more nice and fuzzy that it did when it was actually happening.

Most of my friends and classmates are now parents, and it's really fun to be an "aunty" to the kids (though I would not like to be called that). Frankly, I really enjoyed chatting with Karthika, and it was amusing to see Muskan getting restless and entering our conversation.

Sometimes I think that if we had no memories of our earlier days, life would be so boring. Even if people say we should not live in the past, I still believe that it's the old memories which keeps us going and push us towards a brighter future.

Saturday, July 30, 2011

Being Human

Don't you find that it is only the people you love and care for the most that can make your life unendurable? Others really don't matter.

Taking the above thought further, if someone close to us does something that is not right (in our eyes), the negative effect is manifold compared to someone else we don't have any attachment to. The action or perceived mistake of the loved one is magnified a thousand times and the effect is felt deep within our heart.

Does that mean we really can't be objective where our loved ones are concerned? We are harsh and very tough on them for things which, in others, would seem forgivable. I would think it's not fair, but then, that's the price one pays for being a human with a heart.

Tuesday, August 9, 2011

Catalysts in Our Life

I was rereading books by Agatha Christie featuring Mr Harley Quinn. For those who are not familiar with the character, Mr Quinn is a mysterious fellow who, just by his presence, makes things happens around him. He doesn't do anything magical. He just asks questions or drops hints, and his questions lead to the unravelling of mysteries or an understanding of unsolved issues. It all happens through the statements and behaviour of those connected with the issue. Looking around, we do see people who act like catalysts and speed up things or add spice to life. They ask intelligent questions, they use their (sometimes overactive) imagination, they think creatively, and it all leads to a totally different view about a situation or an object. Life is exciting because of their presence. New things materialize because of them. Most of these things are positive and exciting, but looking at them from another angle, these individuals may also be the ones who cause trouble; they may throw stones in otherwise still and calm waters and try to point out issues where there are none. They may provoke people and make them do things which are harmful. Not only history but day-to-day life is full of such people.

It's important to be able to identify the difference between positive and negative catalysts in our lives. One can drive us to better life, the other towards a negative spiral.

Tuesday, August 09, 2011

Pure Passion

You will never "find" time for anything.

If you want time, you must make it. – Charles Bruxton

We see a large number of people, who just can't "find" time to do a lot of things they would like to do. They wonder how some people "find" time to indulge in what they love to do in this busy world. They think, "Maybe those people are single and don't have family responsibilities, or maybe their work is too easy or light." What they don't realize is that if someone wants to do something, he or she will manage it somehow.

The quote by Charles Bruxton is so true in this context. If one wants to really do something, one can find time by juggling priorities, rescheduling, etc. What is required is a strong passion for the thing one wants to do. If the passion is not there, then there are always excuses for not doing a certain thing.

All around me I see people who lead busy and successful professional lives and still manage to find time for things they are passionate about. I saw this in action during a recent charity show in Hong Kong featuring Bollywood dancing, belly dancing, and Kuchipudi (an Indian classical dance form).

My manager is learning Kuchipudi, which is by no means easy, and she performed for the first time as part of the show. She has to practice a number of hours after long days at work, and she still manages to do quite a few stage shows; this takes commitment, patience, and time management. Her performances (Kuchipudi and the ones based on Bollywood numbers) are quite good, which I as an Indian really appreciate and enjoy.

Of course, all these wonderful performances are only possible because she has a burning passion for dance. It just goes to show that time constraints and busy schedules mean nothing if you really want to do something.

We can safely conclude that if you are not able to "find" time for a particular hobby or activity, it may just mean that you are not passionate enough about it.

Monday, August 22, 2011

Don't Let Them Go

I have lived in cities with millions of people around, and every day this sea of humanity keeps on increasing. Yet I sometimes marvel at the very few people with whom I have a real conversation. Not that I am a wallflower and do not speak to people on my own – I can talk nineteen to the dozen, and I am capable of making small talk. It's just that I can count the people I find interesting to talk to on my fingertips. Some take time to open up and get involved in deep conversations; with others, it's a matter of seconds before you delve into topic after topic and you never seem to stop.

I guess finding someone who can stimulate your thinking, listen to you patiently, and hold your attention for a long period of time is not an easy task. So once you find those people, don't let them go away from your life … ever!

Sunday, August 28, 2011

Names Have Power

There's a saying that "Words have meaning and names have power." I guess it's true; that's why some buildings in Hong Kong are named in an interesting way. I've gotten in the habit of looking at the names of the buildings in HK, and they never fail to amuse me. Some of the ones which caught my attention include:

- Wise Mansion (this building is able to make good choices and decisions)
- Right Mansion (this building is always correct)
- Prosper Gardens (this one says "grow and do well")
- Valiant Park (this building is very brave and determined)
- Happy Gardens (self-explanatory)
- Blessings Garden (in this building, the residents feel grateful)
- Balmy Court (a pleasant and gentle building)
- Rich Mansion (self-explanatory)
- Serene House, Serenity Park (it's a peaceful place)
- Lucky Court

These are real names of buildings. Maybe they were named so that the inhabitants of the particular buildings would acquire those characteristics. But what about names like:

- Still Mansion (does it means motionless, or stagnant or quiet?)

- Ambrosia (it is the food of God)
- Pierce View (seems like a harsh word to me)
- Mellow Mansion (does it refer to serene and peaceful, or ask the inhabitants to calm down and relax?)
- Duet (do people in the building sing duets?)
- Makeway View (what do you think it means?)
- The Sound (?)
- Vibes (good vibes or bad vibes?)
- Rednaxela Terrace (it's the name Alexander written backwards)

Interesting, but are they appropriate? There must be a story behind the naming of these buildings.

Saturday, September 3, 2011

That Extra Mile

One day, I was cribbing to my friend about walking uphill to my house from the gym after heavy sessions thrice a week. She listened to me patiently and had one profound statement for me: "It is this extra mile which will make all the difference." That one line stuck to me like glue. Every time I wanted to give up on something, this statement would come to haunt me, and I would make that final effort to get things done.

Really, that one line does make a difference. It's very true that a high percentage of human beings give up on things when they are very close to achieving the desired result. Make that extra bit of effort, whether it's

- not eating those three or four French fries
- getting up half an hour earlier to avoid delays
- reading your mail one last time to scan for mistakes before sending it off
- doing the last bit of research to ascertain the facts are 100 per cent correct before making a case
- not buying yet another dress
- walking that extra mile home from the gym instead of taking a cab

The extra mile in all walks of life does make a difference.

Tuesday, September 03, 2011

Your Destination Will Find You

Having spent a long time in the corporate world and in human resources, I've always subscribed to the philosophy that if you know your destination, you can always find a way to reach it. Goal-setting has its advantages. It's also true that if you don't know where you're going, you may end up somewhere else.

However, some circumstances do force me to think of another angle. Isn't it possible that if you keep doing what are you are best at and do it passionately, the destination which suits you best will find you on its own? It's like when you are searching using Google, you have options of "Google Search" or "I'm Feeling Lucky." We have all heard that life favours those who help themselves – or in this case, love what they do.

Tuesday, September 13, 2011

Life Is Like a Glass of Bellini

With clear instructions on how to make a glass of classic Bellini, you would expect the taste to be the same everywhere. Surprisingly, it is different everywhere. Some use fresh peach, and it is to die for. Some use peach puree (not fresh) and some use syrup, in varying degrees. The result is not the same anywhere.

The same is true of life. One would expect everything in life to happen the same way as it has in the past in similar situations – but of course, it is not the same. The twists never fail to turn up at the most unexpected moments. Maybe that's what makes every day a new day!

I look at every day of life like a glass of Bellini in an unknown bar. You never know if you are going to like it.

Sunday, September 25, 2011

Really Refreshing

Watching serious movies in-flight is really very tedious for me. In a dazed state while travelling, I am unable to focus on films which require me to concentrate hard. Hence, I naturally gravitate towards animated movies, which are so refreshing. They are not only well-made but also have something for us to take away and remember.

The last one I saw was *Lilo and Stitch,* and the cute characters, storyline, and witty dialogue delivered in a powerful way emphasized the fact that "nobody gets left behind in a family." It left me with a light heart and a wide smile on my face. I have seen very few animated movies, but I still remember *Up, How to Tame Your Dragon,* and the latest Smurfs movie. Every time, I leave with the same good feeling.

Really, these so-called cartoons have a much better impact than the convoluted scripts we see in some of the "grown-up" movies.

Saturday, October 01, 2011

It's True

If there was no compulsion to eat, some human beings would never get out of bed. I learnt that today as a first-hand experience, as I was the human in question. Today being Saturday, I had no pressing need to get up in the morning. I slept for quite some time and finally, when the rumble in my stomach could not be ignored and started giving me a headache, I had to force myself to get up and prepare something to eat. Lo and behold, once the morsels met my stomach juices, the headache disappeared completely.

It made me wonder — if I hadn't needed to feed my grumbling stomach and gain energy, would I just have slept the whole day?

Saturday, October 01, 2011

A Tale of Every City

Every place has its own charm. Whether it's a bustling financial centre or a remote calm and serene place, each one is unique. We all get caught up in discussions of which environment – country, city, or town – is better, and we try to give our reasons. I have done this many times; most recently in a comparison of Singapore and Hong Kong (I favoured HK).

If you go deeper, however, all countries, cities, and towns really have their own positives. Whether it's a quaint small river in the middle of a city; the picturesque view from your apartment; a mélange of sea, land, and mountains; skyscrapers and colourful nightlife; never-ending shopping malls; gardens by the seaside; historical monuments; old-fashioned corners; lovely flowers; the vibrant population, crowded restaurants, beautiful people – all touch the heart of visitors, albeit in different proportions.

While pondering over this, I discovered that for me, all places are charming and worth living in.

Mukta Arya

Wednesday, October 05, 2011

An Interesting Journey:
Mid-Levels Escalator in HK

A modern machine drags noisily through a gathering of unexpected shops selling clothes, shoes, sandwiches, odd furniture, hats, music lessons, spa sessions, foot massages, and Cuban cigars. That's what one experiences when embarking on the Mid-Levels Escalator on Hong Kong Island. It's a curious and engaging way to climb a hill in the middle of the bustling city.

Constructed in 1993, Hong Kong's Mid-Levels Escalator is the longest outdoor covered escalator system in the world. It covers over 800 metres in distance and rises over 135 metres from bottom to top. Whenever I use the escalator (which happens quite frequently), the small shops and their displays never fail to amuse me. Not only is it an entertaining trip, it's hugely educational. The escalator provides the perfect platform for seeing young musicians in action, amateur painters trying their hands on canvas, and women getting their feet massaged. There are rows and rows of shoes with matching handbags in shop windows almost touching the escalator, curiously shaped furniture piled in strange ways, a number of property-management shops with formally dressed salespeople, and numerous bars and restaurants filled with customers at almost all times of the day.

The escalator also provides an opportunity to observe people of all shapes and sizes making their way to their destination – some hurriedly climbing the escalator with lot of energy, some standing on it in a weary way, and some excited by the sights and sounds all around. It's quite interesting that every time I travel on the escalator, there's a different thing which captures my attention. The scene seems to change almost every day, reminding me that life goes on.

Saturday, November 19, 2011

Feedback

It's that time of the year again: appraisal and feedback time. I read somewhere that "People ask for feedback, but they want only praise." It's 200 per cent true. One cannot fathom how true it is until feedback by peers, colleagues, and managers happens to them.

Not so long ago, I got extremely defensive and agitated when I received what HR called "constructive criticism" during an appraisal – or even when well-meaning friends would tell me about areas I needed to improve on. Being an HR person myself and exposed to a number of training programmes on giving and receiving feedback, I did realize that this is my weak area – and I did improve (over a considerable period of time). I liked to think that nothing could bother me. The reality, however, was that even after a lot of soul-searching and convincing me that others will give me frank feedback that human instinct of trying to find negative reasons for that feedback tended to creep in.

The words "constructive criticism" wandered in my thoughts a number of times after that appraisal, and only with great difficulty could I convince myself that the feedback was indeed true and needed some action. Really, receiving feedback and taking it positively is definitely something which requires a lot of self-talk and control. I wonder how saints and some people manage to handle the feedback without feeling perturbed or looking disturbed.

Sunday, November 27, 2011

Pause

It's so important to relax, look back, and take stock of things instead of going full speed ahead in life. The word *review* is so meaningful, not only in corporate life but also in personal life. I time and introspection are important so we can make sure we are doing the right things the right way at the right time to reach our small and big goals.

Really, it's not difficult to find quiet time, even if you are surrounded by a large number of people. You can grab some while walking in the early morning or late at night, while taking a shower, while exercising, while taking breaks at work, while travelling – the opportunities are numerous, and the advantages are more numerous still in terms of focusing efforts and time. Pause, reflect, and then move ahead.

Tuesday, November 29, 2011

Pleasant Surprises

Pleasant surprises do exist, in this very world. The feelings they evoke are, well … *nice*. It's a nice feeling, for example, when you expect nothing out of a meeting and you leave it feeling a sense of achievement; when you don't expect people to behave in a certain way and they do exactly that; when a normally reserved person opens up and tells you incidents about his childhood; or when you meet someone after a long time and don't have words to express yourself, but the silence seems to say a lot.

It's nice to have these pleasant surprises once in a while.

Thursday, December 01, 2011

Women of Substance

A delicious lunch of dim sum started with the normal chatter among the four of us – all of us colleagues, current and former. After placing our order, we sipped at our cups of Chinese tea as the topic turned to maids in Hong Kong. Managing them seemed to be a difficult task. My fellow diners were all young mothers, and for the next hour, the discussion at our table centred on the attracting and retaining of talented maids.

Seems like a banal topic, but what surprised me was that after knowing two of them for more than a year and one of them for half a year, I had never imagined that these women who were so professional and confident in the workplace could go through so much at home in terms of managing their various roles. At work, they were the perfect example of committed employees. One would think that what mattered most to them work was. I hadn't seen even a glimpse of their home life in all these months. Suddenly I heard the various concerns, responsibilities, juggling of priorities, and much more.

I felt lucky to be single and not have the responsibility of looking after a family in Hong Kong, but at the same time, I couldn't help admiring the grit, tenacity, and capability of my professional colleagues, who took multiple competing priorities in their stride, with a broad smile, almost every day.

Sunday, January 08, 2012

All Things Natural

There are many charming and world-famous man-made attractions that people flock to year after year. The beautiful buildings, the towering hotels, and the gravity-defying edifices all command an admiration of humanity's abilities. However, I have noticed that the natural wonders of the world and the breathtaking beauty of nature have a far greater number of admirers – the mountains, valleys, and winding rivers; the remorseless sea with an abundance of sea life; the penguins and seals; the lions and leopards in their natural surroundings; the trees, termite hills, and bird's nests; the volcanoes and hot-water geysers. Even furniture and goods made of natural products are highly valued.

What does this all tells us? I believe the message is that artificiality and pretension may be attractive for a while, but it is to everything natural and genuine that human beings ultimately turn for real enjoyment and peace of mind.

Tuesday, January 31, 2012

Circumstances

The placid waters of the river harbour deep secrets. So still, so peaceful – almost giving the impression of a content life – the water stretches on and on, and a feeling of calm envelopes the mind. We wish our life was as unruffled as the waters.

As we glide by the stretch of water, the serenity is invaded by a sound of urgency – an invasion of silence, the sound of water falling from a height – and the unruffled water becomes furious, falling with intensity. Determined to survive, it emerges from the turmoil victorious.

It makes one wonder whether the way people react depends on circumstances. Perhaps it's the situation which makes a person calm, ferocious, restless, or angry.

Saturday, February 04, 2012

Bling Really Makes Me Sing

The shops in Hong Kong glitter with every type of bling imaginable. Phone covers, bags, clips, purses, iPad covers – you name it, they have it. You'd think the glitter could actually kill a person with the combined strength of its colourful rays.

I always used to wonder who the target buyers for these were really; really bling-y articles which seem to be shouting so boldly *look at me!* Why would someone actually buy these in-your-face things? Well, guess what? I was in for a surprise, a very big surprise. In my own workplace, which is a bank (and therefore, as stereotypes go, should be non-bling-y), I found at least ten of my colleagues – in client-facing and employee-facing jobs – showing a penchant for all things bling. The bling-y items like phone covers didn't really look that bad at all. In fact, they seemed to look quite good and suited the individuals toting them. I asked my colleagues how they became attracted to the glitter and they said, "Just like that!"

Now, when I see these shops, I don't discount them. I actually look at the various designs, marvelling all the while that there's always someone who likes them passionately enough to buy them. Is it that what is bizarre for one is perfectly normal for the other?

Saturday, February 04, 2012

Shortcuts

The truth is that there are no shortcuts in life. Whatever you want to do, whatever you want to achieve, you have to go through the foundation, the basics, and the advanced steps before it's done properly. Shortcuts in life do not exist, *period*.

There are examples of people taking shortcuts, but these are not sustainable. It's like becoming a doctor after taking a six-month crash course. Would you go to such a doctor? Do you think such a person is qualified to be called a doctor? If you read the executive summary of a book, would you be qualified to write a critique of the entire work? I don't think so.

So stop getting lured by so-called shortcuts for studying, for acquiring a skill, for progressing in your career, for losing or gaining weight – in fact, for just about anything. Go through the proper step-by-step process, and you will never regret it.

Saturday, February 04, 2012

Tell Me Why?

There's so much beauty in this world, at every nook and corner, but …

Why do we keep looking at the ugliness and the deep dark secrets?

What pleasure does anyone get out of it?

Why do we look at the weaknesses of others and insist they should overcome those weaknesses?

Why can't we look at the strengths and make sure that they build on strengths instead?

Why do murder mysteries enthral us?

Why do scandals keep us interested?

Why do gossip magazines survive?

Why do we run after what is seemingly unachievable?

Why do we take people who love us for granted?

Why do we like those who seem to have no interest in us?

Why do we realize the importance of something or someone when it's too late?

Why do we waste time assuming and getting it all wrong?

Why do we always want to be someone else?

Why do whine about what we don't have and forget what we have?

Why we are never satisfied?

The questions are endless.

Why? Tell me why?

Saturday, February 25, 2012

The Extraordinary Difficulty of Making a Choice

Have you come across people who take a long time to study the menu in a restaurant or bar and make a detailed study of each item, all the while storing bits and pieces in the decision-making part of their brain? I have promised not to name some of them who I know, but I am sure you have come across such detail-oriented individuals. It's an amazing experience sitting with them in a restaurant and seeing them go through the various offerings of food and drink, making some comment on the ingredients, moving on to another one which catches their fancy (but in a systematic way so that they don't miss anything), commenting again, and finally making a choice. Sometimes, when they are unable to choose, they will ask for help – and sometimes, when the dish or drink is not according to their taste, they wonder why they didn't order something else.

What makes me laugh is the opinion they ask of others as to what is good or not. They forget the basic fact that everyone is unique and has different tastes, so what they find good may not pass the mark for someone else, and vice versa. Give them fifteen or twenty minutes, and they are content to go through the ritual. Distract them by talking about something else, and they will end up making a wrong choice. You will certainly be blamed.

It is my observation that my friends who are in jobs which require very sharp attention to detail are more prone to this behaviour – such as professionals in audit, compensation, benefits, and operations. Hats off to them!

Saturday, March 10, 2012

There's a Time for Everything

In today's world, everyone wants everything right now. *Instant* is the buzzword on everyone's mind. I realized it in Hong Kong and also in Mumbai. Nobody wants to wait.

With advanced technology, patience has become a thing of the past. We call friends on the phone, and if they don't pick up, we don't wait and call back later; we leave a voicemail, or we send an email or SMS. We don't want to climb stairs because there are lifts and escalators. We don't want to walk because there are cars, taxis, and buses. We don't want to go to our colleague's desk because we can communicate through online messages or mail. We don't want to go out to a cafe or restaurant because most places have delivery to our homes and offices. We don't want to cook because there's frozen food all ready to heat up. We don't want to count mentally because calculators have numbed our minds. We don't want to wait for our next promotion; all around us people climb corporate ladders quickly, and we don't want to be left out.

Has patience really become obsolete? If it has, this has not done humankind any favours. We have become a world of impatient, stressed-out individuals with information overload and an inability to do anything for a period of time. We have morphed into restless beings who want to do one thing after the other, without pausing to admire or appreciate what we have already done or have. The world of instant gratification has made us grow up fast, without going through the necessary growing pains. Burnt-out youngsters or people in responsible positions who are unable to cope with the responsibility are sad examples of what happens when we don't spend enough time sharpening the axe before we go to cut a tree. The age-old practice of preparation before doing something seems to have disappeared.

Why don't we realize that time spent in learning is not wasted but actually prepares us for the future? Patience is still a virtue. There's a time for everything.

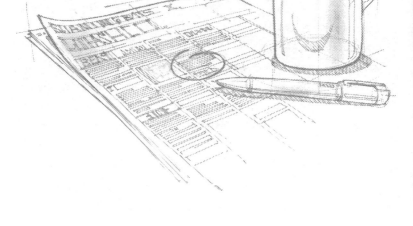

Saturday, May 19, 2012

Those Moments ...

It could be a brief phone call or a quick coffee during the day or a hurried drink after work – just a quick ten to fifteen minutes – but the impact is so high. I'm talking about those few moments you snatch from a busy schedule to share ups and downs with your friends. A few words or sentences are enough to perk you up or push your energy level to where it needs to be. In my experience, these moments act like a vitamin and a catalyst to move myself forward.

These small doses work quite well for me, whether I am in Mumbai or Hong Kong. I recommend them highly to everyone.

Saturday, May 26, 2012

Horoscopes

Leo

Your horoscope for 26 May 2012:

"You are quite likely to enjoy the change in the rhythm and quality of life that is beginning right now, Mukta ... blah ... blah ... blah ..."

Yes, that's what my daily horoscope says for today. I subscribe to my daily horoscope and daily tarot reading via email and never fail to read it. Even though I know that these are generic horoscopes and cannot be true from any angle, I still read them diligently. I confess that as soon as they land in my inbox, I drop everything and read them first. When I pick up a newspaper or magazine, the first column I look for is the one devoted to horoscopes. It's an involuntary action and has been my common practice for a long time now.

More than that, I sometimes go back to my horoscope at night to figure out if my day went as described. I buy the yearly horoscopes at the beginning of the year and then, at the end of the year, do a kind of review. I do try to justify some of the happenings, even when the horoscope is completely off the mark.

Amazing, isn't it? I am educated and know very well that horoscopes can't be true. There are millions of Leos on this earth, and the mailer is targeting all Leos.

I guess it's just human nature to try to figure out what's going to happen in the future and nothing to do with me as a person.

Sunday, July 22, 2012

Hard to Get Bored

I don't know how to get bored – the world has so many interesting things to offer at any given point in time. I remember my childhood, when we didn't have the Internet and video games. There were still so many things to do: cycling, playing outdoor games, reading comics, climbing trees, gardening, and roaming around in the sweltering afternoons inventing games. Every day was a new day.

We grew up, and there were more things: making new friends, visiting new places, discovering love, taking parts in competitions, creating new outfits by cutting the existing ones, spending time in the library finding material for a project, eating out, reading more and more books, spending time with friends – the list is endless.

Every day, human beings and nature create a new outlet for fellow beings to revel in. Whether we're walking through the vistas presented by nature; going to theatres, operas, dance shows, concerts, movies, or art exhibits; writing poetry or prose; or just sharing a glass of wine with a friend, life never fails to spring happy surprises on us.

Friday, July 27, 2012

Light a Candle

"It's better to light a candle than to curse in the darkness." Nothing illustrates the point of moving forward in life like this Chinese proverb, which I saw in a magazine in Hong Kong

We often complain about the unfairness of life – about the doom and gloom of a situation, about this and that – and generally let negativity enter our being.

Is it really worthwhile to feel so beat down? Better to see the bright things in life and smell the roses.

Saturday, November 24, 2012

Elephants Never Forget

People say it's great to have a good memory, like an elephant – and elephants never forget. But is it really that great? I remember a lot of things from the time I became aware of my surroundings as a child:

- the park in which we played as young children
- the trees we plucked fruits from
- the maths teacher I hated in primary school and the Hindi teacher who loved me
- the incidents in various cities we lived in
- the good times and the depressing times
- some of the terrible dreams I had and could never forget
- people who were so nice to me and a few terrible people I came across
- wonderful moments which I would like to remember forever and really miserable moments which I hope would never appear in my life again

At school, university, and work, my memory was a great advantage; I could remember all sorts of important information.

However, there's a downside to retaining so many memories. It's nice to store away the good ones, but the terrible ones are also there, and no matter how much I would like to forget unpleasant occasions and people, they just don't go away.

They pop up whenever there's an association. For me, the saying about forgiving but not forgetting is really true.

It's not exactly great to have memory like an elephant! I wish my brain could do the filtering and delete all the memories except the pleasant ones.

Epilogue

Some of my memories of Hong Kong were also written in the form of poems, which have already been published in two separate books- "Wanton Thoughts" in 2013 and "3:15 pm- Musings in Hong Kong" in 2014.

We are in 2016, and I am still able to find many interesting things in my day-to-day life in Hong Kong. Every day is a new day in this vibrant place.

Printed in the United States
By Bookmasters